Bowed Down to the Dust

Glimpses of Steadfast Love and Faithfulness

BY NIKKI HURT

MISSIONAL PRESS
-NASHVILLE, TN-

© 2021 by Nikki Hurt

ISBN: 978-1-7362821-2-0

All rights reserved. No part of this publication may be reproduced, distributed, or transmitted in any form or by any means, including photocopying, recording, or other electronic or mechanical methods, without the prior written permission of the publisher, except in the case of brief quotations in critical reviews and certain other noncommercial uses permitted by copyright law.

Cover design by Katie Shull.

Published by:
Missional Press, a subsidiary of 610Media.
Nashville, TN
missionalpressbooks.com

Printed in the United States of America.

Bowed Down to the Dust

Glimpses of Steadfast Love and Faithfulness

BY NIKKI HURT

Foreword by Andrea Griffith

i

Foreword

I met my soon to be friend, Nikki Hurt, at a Nancy Leigh DeMoss Wolgemuth live recording in 2009. My husband and I had just planted Gospel City Church in Granger, Indiana, a small town near South Bend, Indiana. In our initial conversation, Nikki's heartbeat for Jesus was revealed. Little did I know during our brief encounter that five years later, Ben and Nikki would come on staff at our church or that several years after that we would send them out as church planters themselves! Years before joining our staff, Ben and Nikki chose to move their entire family to Illinois simply because they had found a church that taught and lived out the gospel. They didn't move for a better paying job or a warmer climate or to be closer to family but so they could sit under and be influenced by the power of the gospel! The seeds for their church, Gospel Community Church in Goshen, Indiana were laid long ago.

Nikki Hurt is a beloved friend and fellow sojourner on the path of life, first, as a Christ follower and secondly, as a pastor's wife. Nikki and I have shared many heart-to-heart talks as we have sought the will of Christ together through blessing and hardship. Nikki has a beautiful story and a gift of writing with authenticity that creates thanksgiving in the heart of the reader. In these pages you will read of a faithful God who reveals His will and His ways in the midst of the ups and downs of life. As a reader you will be encouraged to know you are not alone in your own journey to seek and trust the Lord. If you are a fellow pastor's wife you will be reminded that many have walked this road before us; and all have found God to be faithful, present, and kind. Nikki has a way of seeing Jesus and showing Him to us through the pages of this book.

Andrea Griffith
Gospel City Church, Granger, IN
Pastor's Wife and Lifeway "Weekend to Remember" Speaker

The Glimpses

Page 1
The Preview

Page 2
The Beginning

Page 7
Pirate Sidewalks, Meetings at the Clubhouse, and the Giver of the Gifts

Page 12
Christmastime, a Target Gift Card, and Brad from UPS

Page 17
Grocery Stores, Refried Beans, and the Glory of God

Page 20
A Fork, A Spoon, and His Loving Kindness

Page 24
Women, Infant, Children and Jewel Osco

Page 28
Intermission

Page 33
A Full-Time Job, DD Coffee, and Another Baby

Page 36
Man of Sorrows Acquainted with my Grief

Page 44
A Broken-Down Car, A Prayer, And an Envelope

Page 48
A Dreaded Call, A Broken Tent, and Special Balloons

Page 55
The East and West Wings of California Avenue

Page 63
New York Street, Knocks on the Door, and a Pile of Rocks

Page 69
A Cloud of Despair, A Tough Conversation, and a New Opportunity

Page 73
Going Back, Moving Forward

Page 81
The Ending

The Preview

"Awake! Why are you sleeping, O Lord?
Rouse yourself! Do not reject us forever!
Why do you hide your face?
Why do you forget our affliction and oppression?
For our soul is bowed down to the dust;
our belly clings to the ground.
Rise up; come to our help!
Redeem us for the sake of your steadfast love!"

Psalm 44:23-26

Bowed Down to the Dust

The Beginning

It was July 2009. Our second born was two months old. We were living in our little yellow home on Tonti Street in South Bend, Indiana. I was delightfully a stay-at-home mom to our two children, and Ben was working as a youth pastor at the church he grew up in. To provide extra income for our needs, we worked a side job of cleaning industrial buildings for a friend's business. It was something we had always done together, but Ben had taken the job on solo ever since Isaac had been born.

I was content and blissfully unaware of what lay ahead as I sat on the couch holding our new baby and waiting for Ben to get home. However, the moment he walked through our front door that warm Saturday evening in July fresh, or rather a little sweaty, from cleaning the Niles building, I knew something was about to happen.

"Nikki, I need to talk to you," he said as he clasped both of his hands behind his head and slowly exhaled.

"What Is It?" I asked, alarm rising in me at his unusually curt tone.

"I think we need to move. I have never felt anything like this. I literally feel like my head is going to explode. I feel certain I will be in sin if we don't go."

I took a deep breath, looked around and asked, "What should we do about our house?"

Our house had been on the market for over six months. We had been planning to sell it and hopefully move into something slightly

Bowed Down to the Dust

bigger since we were continuing to grow our family. I loved our 900-square-foot bungalow that sat just north of the St. Joe River, but after five years we were ready to move on. If our house sold while we were considering relocating, then we couldn't make an offer on something local like we had planned. I was concerned about being rushed into a decision simply by accepting an offer on our house.

"Let's get through these two showings that are scheduled for the weekend, and then we will take it off the market while we figure out what we need to do," Ben responded.

We had walked all over our North Shore Triangle neighborhood the past two years talking and praying about this potential move. But somehow it still seemed like this mystical option to me. What is important to note here is that my husband is not a risk-taker by nature. He is steady. He has a tendency, like many of us, to struggle with fear. His statement, *my head is going to explode if we don't do this*, was simply not something he would normally say. It made me lean in close to listen.

That night set off a series of events wherein my 29-year-old self would experience the Lord in ways that I could not have imagined before it all started. A few days later Ben began praying for the Lord to put me on the same page as him. It's not that I wasn't willing to go, but rather that I *needed* to hear from the Lord that this was indeed His plan for us. He prayed all day that the Lord would lead me. Convinced in his own mind of what we needed to do, he wisely knew that I needed to get there on my own.

That night I woke up around 2:00am to nurse Isaac. I went into the living room and turned on a local Christian TV show. The show was known for its interview segments, but it was something that I rarely ever watched, let alone at 2:00 in the morning! A female broadcaster was being interviewed that night and was sharing about a move that she and her husband had made. She discussed how difficult it was for her family but how much they had experienced God through it. Curled up in the recliner in our living room while cradling Isaac and listening to this woman share, I asked God to fill my heart with faith if He was calling us to a similar story. Unbeknownst to me,

Bowed Down to the Dust

Ben lay in our bed fervently praying for the Lord to change my heart. Throughout the whole night, he was petitioning God while I assumed he was sleeping.

The next day he went to the church office early in the morning, and I awoke with a calm that I hadn't experienced before. Recalling the woman's words from the night before, I picked up the phone and called my husband, "It's my turn to tell you something...I think that I could move. I think that God wants me to trust Him and do this with you." He told me later that he nearly dropped the phone.

That short phone call initiated a series of events that rapidly escalated. Those weekend showings that we were supposed to just get through turned into the first reasonable offer we had received on our house in six months. That discussion with our senior pastor where Ben was just going to share his heart ended up with him essentially turning in his resignation. We began having hard conversations with many loved ones and friends. We were both locals to the Michiana area. All of our families lived within 20 minutes of us, simply unheard of in a ministry life. And we are close with both of our families. Our kids adored their grandparents, many aunts, uncles, and cousins. The impending departure was painful. Even harder was attempting to explain to others that we weren't even sure where we were going or what we were doing. We fully confess to the apparent absurdity.

"Do you have a job lined up?"

"Not yet."

"Where will you move to?"

"Either Pennsylvania or Illinois. There is a family of churches that has a pastor's college, and we are going to attend one of their churches."

"Oh, so you are getting a job at another church?"

"No, we are just moving to become part of the church."

"Oh, so you are going to their college for pastors?"

"We hope to, but not necessarily."

If I have led you to believe that I was full of faith over this decision and brimming with excitement and joy over the possibilities, then I

Bowed Down to the Dust

have failed in my communication. I knew I had to follow; the Lord had made that clear to me. But my knees were shaking at basically every moment of the day. My heart was filled with far more fear than faith. I began to recite a short prayer as I started to pack up our beloved little house and prepare to leave it and the town that I had called home for my entire life, "Lord, be there when we leap." It was a simple prayer, repeated over and over, based on a desire to find the Lord faithful when we made this leap of faith into our future.

The Lord can use many ways to speak to his children and calm our fears. Most often it is His Word, alive and active. Sometimes it is through prayer and communion with Him. Other times it is through a trusted friend or member of His body who encourages with the right word, at the right time. And sometimes it is through an old tattered devotion book where the assigned daily reading, written nearly a hundred years before, just so happens to line up with the prayers of the 29-year-old woman doing her best to walk in obedience and trust the Lord for her family's future, "Indeed, there is nothing God will not do for those who will dare to step out in faith onto what appears to be only a mist. As they take their first step, they will find a rock beneath their feet."[1]

---

[1] Cowan, L. B. and James Reimann, Streams in the Desert, p 275.

Bowed Down to the Dust

Saying goodbye to Tonti street.

Bowed Down to the Dust

Pirate Sidewalks, Meetings at the Clubhouse, and the Giver of the Gifts

In October, we stepped out into the mist, hoping to find that rock beneath us and moved our little family to Aurora, Illinois. We had been driving two hours one way to attend Sovereign Grace Church (now Redeemer Community Church) in Oswego since August. We had closed on our house and moved into my parent's basement while we prayed and searched out our next steps. When Ben was offered a part-time, on-call position with a carpet cleaning and water restoration business, we determined that a combination of those hours, along with the tiny amount of savings from the sale of our house, and the severance package that our church in South Bend so graciously offered us would be enough to get us started in our new life.

So the four Hurts moved into an apartment complex in between Ogden (34) and 59 in Aurora. Culture shock ensued. Aurora, and all the surrounding suburbs, was Grape Road at Christmastime, on steroids, all year long. We would drive 30 minutes to simply go three miles. My sister, Stephanie, came to visit early on and forlornly commented, "There is so much concrete everywhere," a far cry from her farm, near the beach in Baroda, MI.

Bowed Down to the Dust

One weekend before we moved, we stayed with a family who also lived in Aurora. The husband spoke about taking the train to work "downtown." Since he lived in Aurora, I assumed he meant downtown Aurora. Why wouldn't I? I grew up in the big city of South Bend, and my mom would often comment about shopping *downtown* at Robertson's for dresses when she was younger. She was, of course, referring to downtown South Bend. I was quite confused then why he would need to take a train to get downtown when he lived so close to it. In a moment of embarrassment, I realized around these parts any mention of "downtown" was, of course, Chicago. I was clearly out of my league here and was only beginning to understand that life was not going to look and feel the same as it once had.

And then there was the apartment complex. To say that living in an apartment with my two children was an unwelcome adjustment for me would be an understatement. Our first night there provided the initial opportunity for a break-down. People from our new church had come and helped us move in. Granted, we had moved from a small house, but moving from even a small house into an apartment is still a big downsize. What do you do with the rakes? The lawnmower? The weed whacker? What do you do with those baby clothes that your newborn has just grown out of but your frugality wants to save for future children? We went to bed overwhelmed by mountains of boxes surrounding us, and I was positive that we would never be able to fit in that place.

A few hours later the boxes were the least of my worries. As my 3-year-old and 6-month-old lay sleeping in the next room, the tenants above us launched a party that I'm confident shook the foundation of the entire apartment building. By God's grace, Ben's knocking on their door asking them to keep it down, and my angry voicemail to the front desk in the middle of the night, the party finally died down in the wee hours of the morning.

In the first few weeks, we quickly began to realize that we needed to find inexpensive ways to entertain ourselves. Reese, our oldest, and I created an imaginary pirate world on the small sidewalks

Bowed Down to the Dust

around the clubhouse. Sweetly innocent of how much her mama was beginning to struggle, she would run excitedly around the building and through the grove of trees onto the *Pirate Sidewalk* exclaiming, "Arrrggg, Matey." The whole apartment complex became like a game to us. We would take walks on our Pirate Sidewalk and chase each other around the tennis courts. We never actually played tennis, but it was a great place to throw and bounce balls. A tennis net is the perfect height for a three-year-old!

We also held special daily meetings. The clubhouse of the apartment complex offered free coffee and hot chocolate at all hours. A few different sections of tables and chairs set up throughout the main lobby afforded super-secret meeting spots for my highly imaginative three-year-old. We would place Isaac in his stroller, pack some papers and pens into a backpack, and follow the Pirate Sidewalk to the clubhouse for our pretend meetings. Hot chocolate and coffee were essential elements as we plotted and planned. The ladies at the front desk would smile at my sweet girl who was so delighted to be living in this apartment complex world with all of its adventures. She was unaware of the tears I hid behind my sunglasses and of the questions that began to surface, "What are we doing here, Lord?" She didn't understand the dwindling income as that part-time, on-call position didn't produce any hours at all our first two weeks in Illinois. Thankfully, Ben also found work as a temporary UPS loader just in time for the holiday season. He woke up extremely early for his shift 30 minutes away in Addison. It was only part-time and seasonal, but at least it was some work, and we were grateful to God for His provision.

One day we were all strolling on the Pirate Sidewalk together as Reese rode her tricycle that we stored in our bedroom closet. As the elm trees lining the sidewalk swayed in the autumn wind, Ben quietly asked me a pointed question, "Nikki, God loves to give us good gifts. But He doesn't want us to delight in the gifts. He wants us to delight in Him. Do you love the gifts? Or do you love the Giver of the gifts?" Of course, I knew the *right* answer to this question. But it exposed my heart nonetheless. I had been in tears all week because we couldn't set up Reese's trampoline, a gift from her grandparents for her 3rd birthday in March. We had never set it up because our house had been on the market, and we were waiting until we moved. I had no idea that we would move to a different state and into an apartment complex, backyard not included!

Our little family of four, visiting South Bend at Thanksgiving after moving to Aurora the month before.

Our path had taken such a different turn than I had planned. And now, as I walked around the concrete jungle of Aurora, my heart grieved that my children could not play in their own backyard. Not only that, but I was completely uncertain if or when they ever would. This wasn't what I had dreamed of when starting our young family. My heart desperately wanted, and most likely even idolized, a certain picket-fenced life. The pirate sidewalks and countless meetings at the clubhouse weren't measuring up in my mind to their own patch

Bowed Down to the Dust

of earth with a swing set near the trees and a trampoline to play on as the sun went down on golden fall evenings.

Thus began a journey, which still continues, of discerning who, or what, I am treasuring. Am I treasuring Christ alone, the one my heart was made to worship? Or am I treasuring an idolized life of picket fences that I think I somehow deserve?

It took living in an apartment complex with my family of four to reveal my heart, and it's taken more years of submitting to Christ and repenting of my sin to begin to peel away the layers of idolatry. It's funny how now, years later, my eyes will still tear up remembering these days. But the tears are no longer for the absent backyard or the unused trampoline. Rather, tears spill over for the pure innocence and sweetness of time with my baby girl, toddling along with pirates and waving to the front desk ladies with her little backpack full of pens and papers. The Lord, in His goodness, truly does give us good gifts.

Christmastime, a Target Gift Card, and Brad from UPS

After settling into our apartment that fall, we immediately joined a small group within our new church. We longed for biblical fellowship and loved the community we witnessed from afar. We wanted to involve ourselves in the life of this body; and if the Lord opened the door, we hoped to be invited to attend their pastor's college in Maryland.

We no longer have regular contact with most people from this small group; but even so, my heart swells with love for these friends. As I sit here, writing this down, I can see each of their faces. They were the hands and feet of Jesus to us for the days, months, and even years to come.

We met at the home of a wonderful family of six who lived in Warrenville. The group, composed of different people from our church, also included a few Wheaton College students from the nearby campus. The need to find childcare for Reese and Isaac so that Ben and I could regularly attend reduced me to tears at our very first meeting when the subject came up. For the first time since becoming a mother, I couldn't rely on any family members to help watch our children. I felt frozen in fear. I didn't know where to look for a sitter, and we were so new to the church that I didn't know who to ask. Three of those Wheaton College students, whom I had just met, volunteered to rotate missing our group, drive the 45 minutes to our apartment, and care for our kids so that we could attend. We were astonished. They selflessly continued this sacrificial service for a few months until we were able to find someone in our church whom we could pay to replace them. It was a tangible glimpse of the Lord's love and faithfulness to us.

During these first few months the work at the restoration company remained unpredictable and infrequent. Sometimes Ben would drive to west Aurora right after the early morning UPS shift, work a full and strenuous day, and then collapse into bed before needing to wake up and do it all again. Those days were very long and tiring, but we thanked God for the provision. Other days he would come home after UPS, not having any other work that day; and we would fight for joy and contentment as he set up Reese's stuffed animals and took her on Nerf gun safaris throughout the apartment.

Throughout this time, he began to develop a friendship with a man named Brad who worked the docks at UPS with him. A rough-around-the edges guy, Brad was not a believer in Christ. And yet the two of them grew to be friends and engaged in many spiritual conversations. Brad was dumbfounded that we had moved when we did, during the 2009 recession, and for the reason that we did, to join a church. Ben invited him to bring his wife over for dinner with us one night; but he declined, stating, "His wife didn't like to do that sort of thing." Early one morning during their shift, Ben was able to share the Gospel with Brad. We have no idea what the Lord has done with that seed in his life. But we do know that the Word of God never returns void. Meanwhile, we were continuing to be invested in by our small group. I'd like to say that we did some sort of investing too, but I fear that would not be accurate! We were beginning to feel quite lost in this life. We were confident that the Lord had called us to move; but once settled, we were at a loss for what to do next. It was shaping up to be an exceptionally confusing time for us.

One afternoon, a couple weeks before Christmas, I took the kids to Target for some essentials. I had planned on Reese wearing a beautiful hand me down dress for Christmas that someone at our

Bowed Down to the Dust

church in South Bend had given her. It had a black velvet top, red satin bow across the middle, and a full black and white plaid skirt. It was stunning. While shopping, I spied a cute black and white plaid headband and a pair of red knitted tights across the Target aisles.

Oh, the war that waged in my soul standing amongst the accessories at Target that morning! I so badly desired them for her. They would have perfectly matched the dress that I already had, and they couldn't have been more than $12 combined. But we were on an extremely tight budget. The part-time UPS gig was clearly not enough for a family of four to live on. We were dependent on Ben getting as much work through the restoration company as possible. But since that had been so irregular, we were blowing through our savings on important things like rent, food, and gas to get back and forth to his two jobs.

No, I could not justify spending money on something so frivolous as a headband and tights. They would have matched perfectly, and she would look adorable, but it just wasn't a need. I asked God to give me grace and contentment, and I walked away.

A few days before Christmas we attended our small group's Christmas party. Our wonderful new friends surprised us with an envelope that read, *For Christmas Fun.* How wise to label it as such! Without that label, I promise we would have spent it on something practical like groceries. They prayed for us and sent us on our way, grateful to be seen and cared for. When we arrived home, we opened it up and found mostly cash; but, lo and behold, there on the top was one singular Target gift card for $25. Oh, I knew just what Christmas fun I would have with that!

Early the next morning the kids and I rushed to the store. Just a couple of days remained before Christmas at this point. My heart sank as I could see that the shelves were picked over and in disarray. But there on the wall of headbands remained one black and white plaid headband, hanging lop-sided on the hook. I grabbed it with a squeal and turned my attention to the tights. At first glance there was nothing. But wait! I glimpsed a bit of red beneath the pile of pink, white, and black.

Bowed Down to the Dust

"Lord, please let these be her size," I silently prayed.

Deep in my heart I knew that they were. He is the God who sees, and He saw my heart and knew the love I had for this little girl and the delight it would be to dress her up so pretty for Christmas morning! I grabbed ahold of the red tights and thanked God for His kindness as I placed them, just her size, in our shopping cart.

During the early dawn hours of Christmas Eve, Ben worked his last shift with Brad. Ben would be staying on as a permanent part-time employee for UPS, but Brad only wanted the job as a seasonal gig. He would be leaving the dock that morning for the last time. As the two guys clocked out, Brad asked Ben to follow him to his car. He unlocked it and brought out two gifts. One wrapped for a little girl and one wrapped for a 6-month-old baby boy—two kids that he had never met. Ben, choking back tears, thanked him for his kindness as they hugged goodbye.

We think of Brad often. We don't know where life has taken him or if he has ever come to see Jesus as worthy of all our praise.

We hope so.

What a truly memorable Christmas the Lord bestowed upon us.

Reese with Grandpa Steve and the last headband, hanging lopsided on the shelf at Target.

Bowed Down to the Dust

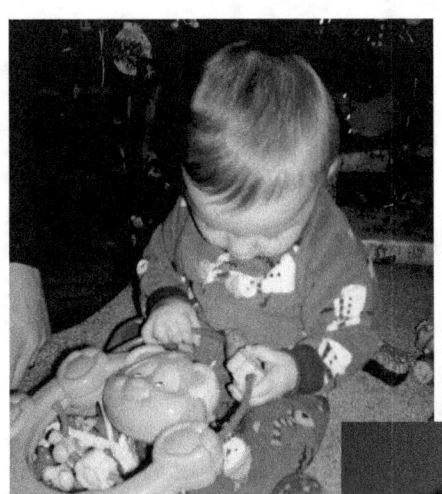

Special gifts from Brad at UPS, a friend they never met!

Bowed Down to the Dust

Grocery Stores, Refried Beans, and the Glory of God

I measure my life by the grocery stores I've shopped at. This may be a result of having moved so many times. It started when Reese was a baby, and I mainly shopped at the Meijer near our church in South Bend where Ben's office was. I adored taking her in to shop with me! She would sit in the front of the cart, and we would play a little game where she would kiss my cheek every time we started down a new aisle. Then we would stop in to see Daddy and Grandma, who worked as the church secretary, before heading home to drop off our groceries.

When we moved, I had to find new stores to shop at. And now I had two little kids to give me kisses up and down the aisles! There were a number of stores that I shopped at in Illinois, but none of them could top Woodmans. Everyone who lives in the northern part of the state knows about Woodmans. Years later we came back to Illinois to visit friends; and my friend, Misha, asked me what I wanted to do. I responded, "I really just want to walk around Woodmans together."

Nowadays, the craze is store pick-up or even delivery to your home. I just can't get on that train. I truly love taking my kids to the grocery store. Yes, it's a little hectic at times to take all five of them with me, though I've done it many times; but nothing beats one on

Bowed Down to the Dust

one time at the grocery store with mom! I bribe them with, "You'll get to pick out the treats"; or I even just pick a couple of the kids and flat out say, "You are coming."

So, as much as I've always loved it, grocery shopping in Illinois was challenging. Maybe one of the reasons I love it so much today is because I can fill our cart with everything we need, and I don't have to be concerned about whether or not we can afford it. It fills my heart with joy to head to the grocery store and buy a cart full of groceries for my family.

During that time of our lives, I regularly served the family pancakes because they are cheap and filling. However, one day, I was so sick of pancakes and wanted to spice it up a bit. I headed to Aldi, across the street from our apartment complex, to buy ingredients for bean burritos! Living it up on Landing Drive!

I bought flour tortillas, a can of refried beans, shredded cheese, and taco sauce. For the first time in my entire life, our checking account bounced because of that purchase. I had miscalculated when Ben would be paid by one day. We still had a little bit in savings that the bank brought over to cover it, but we were still charged some fees for the bounced check. Even though no one knew about it, I was humiliated, angry, and ashamed.

I didn't understand why God was allowing us to be brought so low that I couldn't even afford a can of refried beans.

"Where are you?" I was screaming internally.

"How is this good? How does this bring you glory when no one even knows the depth of our situation here. No one knows that we can't afford a can of beans!"

And then the Holy Spirit spoke to my heart in such a profound way. I can still recall the moment standing over the stove, stirring those beans, when it happened.

"I know," He answered.

And in a flash I understood. I had always looked at Matthew 5:16 as the primary way that the Lord received glory, "In the same way, let your light shine before others, so that they may see your good works and give glory to your Father who is in Heaven." So how then,

Bowed Down to the Dust

in a situation that no one could see or even knew about, could God be glorified? It was in that moment that I understood the Lord wanted *my heart* to glorify him. He didn't intend to be glorified solely by shining a light before men, "Make thankfulness your sacrifice to God, and keep the vows you made to the Most High. Then call on me when you are in trouble, and I will rescue you, and you will give me glory" (Psalm 51:17).

He had my heart at the point of my salvation. He became my Savior *and* my Lord. I was alive to do His bidding. But the Lord also wanted to be *glorified* through my attitude and the posture and inclination of my heart, not simply by good works that could be observed by others. In any and every situation that I was in, I could say, "Yes, Lord, have your way;" and if this was the position of my heart, then He would be glorified, even if not a single other person alive was aware of it. Jesus would be aware of it!

I don't need others watching me in order to bring glory to God. I have an audience of one, and He is glorified when my heart submits to Him. What freedom that one can of refried beans ended up bringing to my soul!

Bowed Down to the Dust

A Fork, A Spoon, and His Loving Kindness

Throughout this difficult season, I was learning that Jesus cared greatly about the inward responses of my heart. I finally recognized that the position of my heart before Him could bring Him praise - even if no one else was around to see it. But, alas, my heart still really missed my husband.

Over 10 years later and this interval of time is still almost impossible for us to talk about without it stirring up great emotion. We went through long stretches of time where we just did not see Daddy. His regular weekly pay was based on carpet cleaning. We needed the late overtime hours and the emergency calls for our real provision. While I was growing up, my dad worked for the power company; and I was used to regulations like mandatory rest times and comped meals. Ben's company never received that memo. He would literally have weeks where he would clock 100 physical labor hours. When he was home, I would try to do everything I could just to allow him some time to relax. He was working very hard for our family, and I was caring for our children and keeping our home as organized as I could.

One night he actually arrived home before it was very dark. We enjoyed a large common area behind our patio at the apartment where our kids would play. It was usually completely empty. This particular evening a man was outside with his child, and our kids started to play a bit. The kids and I had already eaten, and the man

Bowed Down to the Dust

came over to talk with us just as I was bringing dinner out to Ben to eat on the patio. The man's eyes widened as he exclaimed, "Can you teach my wife to do that?!" Ben smiled awkwardly and continued chatting with the man despite his exhaustion.

Many other times Ben would call late in the afternoon. "I'm not gonna make it home before the kids go to bed," he would say. "If you can meet me out here, I can leave for a bit to eat dinner with you guys." We would jump in the car and drive to a random Chipotle somewhere in the Chicago-land area just to see him for a few moments that day. Reese and Isaac would leap from their car seats and run to him. We consumed a lot of quesadillas and tortilla chips in order to see Daddy while we lived in Illinois, not that I'm complaining about that part.

On top of all that, the emergency calls often pulled him away from us. The company established a rotating on-call schedule. The on-call pay was the 3rd tier–the best of the best. If you received a call during that time, you made very good money. It was impossible to pass up, not that he would be allowed to anyway. I can't count the number of times we had plans that needed to be cancelled because Ben got a call right as we were walking out the door or the number of times that he missed visiting with my parents or his after they had made the trip to visit us.

Throughout all of this, the Lord knit us together. We developed a strong team mentality. I realize the situation had the potential to fracture our relationship, and there certainly were times of great stress; but overall, and by the grace of God, we were a united front. It truly felt like it was us against the world, and we were determined to stick together and win.

At times, though, I would lash out in my confusion, "Why are we doing this? *What* are we doing? Do you want to be in ministry or not?" A big part of me wanted to throw in the towel on this whole adventure, send out some resumes to some random churches across the country, and be done. Looking back, I can see the Holy Spirit restraining Ben from doing just that. He would always look at

Bowed Down to the Dust

me and say, "It's just not the right time. I don't know what God is doing, but He is working here. We have to keep trusting Him."

I am confident there were days that I made life extremely hard for my husband. I'm sure it was tempting for him to quit when the days were so long, and he knew that I was becoming so unhappy. Not that ministry is particularly an easy life, but I figured at least we would have had a little more direction and tangible purpose. I struggled immensely with the sense of the unknown that was such a requirement of our current path. *Will our church ever decide to send him to the pastor's college? Will he ever get another opportunity to be in ministry? How long will he have to stay in this job and work such an unpredictable schedule?*

We loved our church and the people in it. We *lived* for Sundays. But we still had to make it through the rest of the week. I can remember many, many small group meetings where Ben showed up late, in his work uniform, having just met me there. Or even a few where he didn't make it at all. The entire reason we moved was to immerse ourselves in this local body, and oftentimes he was kept from it.

So, yes, we were mostly a united front, but there were also times of great fear, confusion, and me begging him to be done with all of this. At the end of those moments, after we had worked it out and prayed together, he would often look at me and say, "I don't know, Nikki, I just really believe the Lord is doing something here, and this is going to mean something someday." God was doing something, right then and there. We were just too much in the middle of the storm to realize that He was actively working things out within us.

All of this came to a head for me one night in Reese and Isaac's bedroom. Ben was gone again. I was so tired and lonely and at a complete loss on what to do with my children after having been alone with them for a long stretch of several days in a row. I had a fork and a spoon, and I created a little puppet show with them. Isaac was giggling his sweet baby laughter, Reese was laughing because he was laughing, and I was fuming on the inside, "Why would you lead us here just for me to be alone all of time?! Why does he have to

Bowed Down to the Dust

work so much, but we still can barely afford to live here?! I don't want to be here anymore! I hate it here!" At that, I threw the fork up in the air. The kids were still laughing, thinking it was part of my show; but inwardly, through gritted teeth, I was raging against the Lord, "If you don't hold onto me, I will leave you," I declared as the fork sailed through the air.

There it was. My faith, hanging on by a thread. I had come to the absolute end of myself. It's funny sometimes the things that will push us over the edge. It seems so small. A puppet show with two laughing kids? A mom who wanted nothing else but to be at home with her kids upset that she now is? In reality, it wasn't the puppet show or the laughing kids. It was all the moments of missing my husband and missing the life that we used to have together that finally came spilling over in one gigantic wave of rage against my Creator.

I spent the rest of that day and night, done with Jesus. It pains me greatly to say that. But it's true. It's as if I were an angry child who slammed the door in His face and then closed her eyes and plugged her ears. I walked away from Him in my heart that night. I still made my kids dinner, read them a story, and hugged and kissed them before bed. But as far as communing with the Lord, I was done.

I woke up the next morning after a hard and deep sleep, alone because Ben was already back to work. In a way I simply cannot describe the presence of God was thick all around me. I actually gasped out loud. It was like He sat there by my bed, keeping watch all night while I slept, holding onto me. The sun was streaming in through the slants of the blinds, creating streaks across the floor and the wall. An indescribable holiness filled the room. I fell to the ground, my face to the floor, in complete repentance, "Forgive me, Lord! Have your way with me. You hold my lot. I will follow you." His loving kindness held me tight and did not let me go. His loving kindness led me to repentance.

I walked away from Him the night before, but *He did not let go of me*. Praise God for my affliction! His loving kindness brought me to repentance, and now I keep His Word (Psalm 119: 67-68).

Bowed Down to the Dust

Women, Infant, Children, and Jewel Osco

I don't recall if it was before the refried bean incident or after, but Ben and I prayerfully decided to sign up for the WIC program provided by the state. We would have qualified for this even when Ben was still a youth pastor, but I must admit that I was too prideful to go through with it then. We both desired for me to stay home with our children, especially while they were still so young. We knew we were sacrificing a second income to do so, but we learned to budget our money well and always sought to live within our means. I had, at times, considered taking on a part-time job; but with the cost of childcare and Ben's extremely unpredictable schedule, it just didn't make sense for our family at the time.

We came to the conclusion that not only did we qualify for this help from our government but that we actually needed it. These programs were created to help low-income women and children; and that, we were finally realizing, was us. Still, I was struggling with some serious pride in accepting the help. I thought, "I'm a college graduate. I don't think college graduates are supposed to be on WIC." It was also a stigma that I picked up on in my family of origin. People like *us,* did not do things like *that.*

God brought other thoughts to our minds that helped me to apply finally. One was knowing that I had worked for seven years before having our kids. So I had, at one time, helped to pay into this system that I would now withdraw from. Also, Ben was working this entire

Bowed Down to the Dust

time and continually paying his taxes. We could have qualified for much more help at that point; but Ben's feeling was, "Let's be conservative and take some of the help offered, but we won't take it all." Hence, the reason for showing up at just the WIC office and not also joining the long line for food stamps.

Ben was determined to go with me to sign up. He did not want me to go through this new and humbling experience on my own. Aurora is the second highest populated city in Illinois outside of Chicago. We were not prepared for the size of this building nor for the number of people within it. We felt ashamed and awkward. We nearly turned around and left. In fact, I recall having the conversation in the car about doing just that, "Do you really want to go through with this?" I said.

"I think it will be a help for us," he replied, "Let's go inside and check things out, and we can leave if we don't feel comfortable."

In hindsight, it's silly how nervous we were. We made it through that first simple meeting without any lasting scars. The receptionists checked our paystubs to make sure that we qualified for the program, we were assigned a nutritionist, and we met with her before leaving with our checks for healthy foods like eggs, whole-grain cereals, fruit, vegetables, beans, rice, etc.

However, if making our way through the initial visit was tough, it was nothing compared to the shaking of my knees, sweaty palms, and raised heart rate of taking those checks to the store for the first time. Only certain stores accepted WIC, and so I headed to my nearest Jewel Osco on 59 in Naperville. It was torture! I felt like I was committing a criminal act. I always thought this sort of thing was for *other people*. It took a big dose of humility to realize that I *was* one of those *other people*.

I truly had no idea what I was doing. I didn't know that I had to line up the groceries on the conveyor belt in order of what was on the check and then place the check with it. I just put it all together on the belt like I had done every other time I had shopped. When the checkout lady realized I was a WIC customer, she was so exasperated with me! I was mortified. I said, "I'm sorry. This is my

Bowed Down to the Dust

first time using these." She offered no compassion. To make sure that I was truly humbled, she proceeded to grab her microphone and call out through the whole store for her manager announcing, "WIC customer on aisle 5! WIC customer on aisle 5!" as the customers all around shuffled their feet and avoided making eye contact with me.

Once we were all squared away and I headed out the door with bags full of groceries, the Lord spoke to my heart again; and my steps became lighter. *The Earth is the Lord's and the fullness thereof.* "Everything in that store belongs to the Lord," I thought. "To some, He gives money through their hard work, and they go into the store and get what they need. To others, He gives a few WIC checks every month, and they go into the store and get what they need. Either way it all belongs to Him, we just fool ourselves into thinking otherwise."

After our initial visit, we would return to the WIC office every six months to update our paystubs, ensuring that we still qualified, and be loaded up again with the checks for healthy foods. I learned the correct way to arrange the food on the conveyor belts at the store, and I always found the nutritionists at the meetings to be kind and welcoming. Over time I began to be genuinely grateful for their help and care as they sought to teach on good nutrition choices. I began actually to enjoy our WIC appointments, and I started to think of it more as a ministry. I looked for ways to encourage and talk to the other moms in the waiting room. Even if it was just a smile or a comment on how adorable their baby was. I also looked for ways to show appreciation to the nutritionists and other staff. I answered their questions the best that I could, and I thanked them for doing their jobs so well.

One of the goals of WIC is to keep mothers nursing their babies through their first year of life. Lower income women do not typically have as high a rate for nursing their babies as higher income women do. WIC hopes to come alongside mothers to offer the support and encouragement needed to sustain breastfeeding for as long as possible, so they will reward moms for nursing by keeping lactating women on the program for longer. You essentially get more food for

Bowed Down to the Dust

your family by nursing for longer. For that reason, I became somewhat of a star at my local WIC office because I continued to nurse Isaac exclusively for his first year.

We had to complete regular classes as part of the program too. Most of these were rather dull and were done online. But one Saturday morning I was required to take part in a breastfeeding class in person. When the instructor realized that I was a participant and that I was still nursing Isaac who was nearing a year old, she unduly praised me in front of all the others. She then directed all of the ladies to ask their questions of me that morning.

"What do you do when your baby falls asleep?" one mom asked.

Another questioned, "How do you know when he is finished?"

I was near to tears as these mothers looked to me to answer their questions; and I left that morning feeling humbled once again, but in a new and different way. I was no longer embarrassed to qualify for WIC or to show up at the office for our appointments. Rather, I was humbled that the God of the Universe would choose to use me to encourage other mothers who loved their babies just as much as I did mine and were looking to provide what their babies needed just like I was. We can find ministry happening in the most wearisome places if we allow ourselves to be humbled enough to show up for it.

Intermission

Lest I lead you astray and cause you to believe that every single day of our lives was filled with misery, I'd like to take a break from the narrative and highlight some of the things we did for fun as a family. Through creativity and the blessing of the simple things in life, we were able to experience some very sweet times as a family during our time in Illinois. Below is a list of ways we kept things light and fun.

Parks

Parks were our absolute best friend. Isn't this true of every young family? In the midst of all the concrete, Illinois is home to some amazing parks and green spaces. Our apartment was near Naperville, which has one of the sweetest downtown areas I've ever visited. We hung out around their quaint riverwalk often. The very end of it empties into one of our most favorite parks. And if Daddy was with us, and tips were good that week, we would definitely get some frozen yogurt at Red Mango or meet our friends the Andersons there on Sunday afternoons.

Bowed Down to the Dust

Libraries
Libraries were our second favorite friend. As a former librarian and lover of all things book related, this will never change! They are great places for families to hang out, meet up with others, take part in programming, and most often all for free. Bonus!

Star Ball Hunts
We used to own a red ball with a yellow star on it. The star sported a friendly smiling face. We lost that thing 100 million times around the apartment complex, and we found it just as many times. Underneath someone's car in the parking lot. Near a bush three buildings over. Underneath the trees of the Pirate Sidewalk. On the tennis courts. It never failed to find us, and it gave us a great many moments of hilarious laughter. Rest in Peace, Star Ball. She has been officially lost for a good many years now.

Fox Valley Mall
It wasn't just Aldi that greeted us from across the street of the apartment complex. Fox Valley Mall also welcomed us! Any mom with little kids knows what a blessing a mall food court is! And this mall possessed a large, 2-story carousel in the food court as well! For just $1 the kids could ride the carousel. When we found out Daddy was working late, off to the mall we'd go to ride the carousel and meander around pushing Isaac in his stroller. One day Reese commented while we pulled out onto 34, "Mommy, how kind of the Lord to put a mall right across the street from us!"

An Invented Game that Has No Name
Ben invented a car game that we sometimes play to this day. It goes like this: One person asks a question and calls it out in a sing-song voice, "If you love Mommy say, 'We Love you, Mommy!'" and everyone repeats in unison, 'We love you, Mommy!'" Then someone

else says something like, "If you love pizza say, 'Mama Mia,'" and everyone shouts, "Mama Mia." Everyone takes turns coming up with his or her own saying, and it produces amazing giggles and sometimes great outbursts of laughter. Often, we would hop in the car just to drive around town and play our game. The only rule was that Daddy had to be with us. We never, *ever* played without Daddy.

Trips Home or Trips to See Us

We would take weekend trips home to see family fairly regularly. We were grateful that even though we moved away it was still only a 4-5 hour round trip. We could even do the trip in one day if we needed to. Our parents often came to see us, and our siblings did a couple of times too. We loved having family come to stay with us. My mom would regularly come just for the day. It was such a huge treat for our kids when anyone came to visit us.

Family Passes

Our greatest splurge every year was a family pass to the Dupage Children's Museum. We loved taking the kids there! We had many friends with passes too, so it was a great place to meet up and spend time together. You bought a pass one time and could go as much as you wanted all year long! This was a life saver for me and the kids when Ben's hours grew crazy. If you want to bless a family with young kids, buy them a pass at a children's museum or nature park! It truly is the gift that keeps on giving.

These were just a few ways that we experienced joy and laughter in the midst of confusing, stressful, and somewhat depressing times. I mean, it really *was* kind of the Lord to put a mall across the street from us!

And now, back to the regularly scheduled days of hardship.

Bowed Down to the Dust

Dupage Children's Museum on Isaac's 1st Birthday!

Bowed Down to the Dust

Bowed Down to the Dust

A Full-time Job, DD Coffee, and Another Baby

By the spring of 2010, we had nearly depleted our finances. Ben was still working the very early morning shift at UPS and was still clocking hours with the restoration company as well. But the nature of the work was so fragile. Some weeks he would work 80+ hours and the next week only 20. The weeks he had overtime the pay was quite good. The problem was both in the inconsistency of it all and in the fact that Illinois has a higher standard of living. We just couldn't ever catch a break. I will add that despite all of this and because of the complete faithfulness of God, we acquired no debt at all the entire time we lived in Illinois. We definitely lived paycheck to paycheck, but we resisted the urge to live above our means.

Nevertheless, the day finally came when I checked our bank account and realized that we would not be able to pay our rent for the first time since moving. We had less than half the amount needed, and rent was due in two weeks. We had been needing to supplement his checks with our savings so often that it finally just gave out. We had no more savings. I sat in my car outside our apartment door and prayed. The peace of God that transcends all understanding wrapped in and out of that vehicle, "Lord, you have promised to never leave or forsake us, and we need to see that right now." The words of King David sifted through my thoughts, "The

Bowed Down to the Dust

steps of a man are established by the Lord, when he delights in his way; though he falls, he shall not be cast headlong, for the Lord upholds his hand. I have been young, and now am old, yet I have not seen the righteous forsaken or his children begging for bread" (Psalm 37:25-26).

The next day Ben came home from his early morning shift carrying a Dunkin Donuts coffee in each hand–the one rare and extravagant treat we allowed ourselves. He punched them both up in the air with the biggest grin of relief I had ever seen spread across his face. The restoration company had finally come through on all of their promises over the past several months. They were offering him full-time with benefits effective immediately. He would be able to turn in his notice at UPS and concentrate on one job.

We celebrated and rejoiced. God had provided. All along the way, the path had been rocky and looked nothing like what we thought it would when we stepped out in faith back in July to follow the Lord's leading. We were stripped of many comforts and lacked much ease in our days. But we simply cannot say that God was not faithful. He was faithful in every single way. The rent came due two weeks later and was once again paid on time and in full.

In retrospect, we could have decided to take it easier at this point and maybe gotten on our feet a bit more. We could have looked to move out of the apartment and at least into a house to rent with a backyard for the trampoline. We probably would have done all of those things except the Lord laid a dream on my heart. That dream was a little girl named Raegan Lenee.

I had just turned 30. I had many friends that struggled with infertility, and we ourselves had experienced two miscarriages before Isaac. I wasn't thinking much about having more children until all of a sudden, I was! It was as if I woke up one morning with the dream of Raegan on my heart. I knew it was crazy. I knew in the eyes of the world it would be considered unwise. We had endured so much financially and were certainly not that much better off even though Ben did have more steady employment.

Bowed Down to the Dust

I set to praying and asking the Lord to prepare Ben's heart for having another baby. I waited for what I thought was a good moment and then shared with him, "I know it seems crazy, but I really want another baby and feel like the Lord is telling me the time is now. We are in our 30s. This is the time to grow our family. I don't want to wait too long and end up struggling to get pregnant. The Lord could change our finances in a heartbeat if He chooses to. I just want to trust Him."

To my astonishment he answered quickly and soundly with, "Okay. I agree. Let's trust the Lord."

We were pregnant with Raegan by the end of that month. Isaac had just turned a year old. While pregnant with her, I remember watching an HGTV show at my parent's house and was so saddened by a couple on the show. They lived in a wonderful 3-bedroom home in a beautiful neighborhood. They were trying to sell it because they wanted to have a second child. They weren't able to sell the home and commented at the end of the show that they were putting off getting pregnant because they wanted to be in a 4-bedroom house before growing their family. I just sat there thanking God that He had guarded our hearts from that way of thinking.

We've endured a fair amount as a family. We've driven battered, rusty cars. We've never taken a trip to Disney World or flown our kids anywhere. But my Raegan is such a gift! She is a walking testament to me of trusting in the Lord and living by faith. Now, in hindsight, we often comment that had we not trusted the Lord and been gifted with Raegan at that time we may not have ever made it to our twins, five years later. My children are my greatest treasures. I agree with being wise and seeking to be good stewards of our finances that God gives to us. But I also look around our messy, loud, full table and know that we are indeed very rich and that the greatest things in life cannot be bought.

Bowed Down to the Dust

Man of Sorrows Acquainted with My Grief

So, there we were pregnant with our third child in the summer of 2010. We were elated. We believed God had ordained her life to begin at that precise moment of time. Even so, I am prone to moments of doubt and uncertainty just like the next person. I remember one such phone call with my sister, Stephanie. Through tears I panicked, "Did we somehow test God? Will this be the moment of time that we do not see His faithfulness?"
She kindly reminded me, "Nikki, you can desire to have a baby, but God is still the one who brings forth life. A baby is not a test. God will be faithful."
One of the ways we needed to see that truth once again was in the realm of health insurance. Ben was offered a policy from his employer but received no coverage for his wife or children. We could buy into it at the full price, but it was astronomical. Like many families post the recession of 2009, we literally had to choose between paying insurance premiums or paying our rent.
I've mentioned that Ben had decided we would accept some help from government programs but not all the help available to us. Our kids had already been enrolled in the state provided health insurance that we paid a small premium for; and with this pregnancy I was eligible to enroll as well. And so entered my foray into the great government healthcare system. I applied and was quickly accepted. In spite of the limited number of options, I found a doctor whose

Bowed Down to the Dust

practice was fairly close to our apartment, and so I called to make my first appointment.

With its pleasant exterior, the office itself seemed fairly typical; and it was close to the hospital where Raegan would be delivered. The inside was clean, though sparse, and the woman at the front desk was kind and approachable. They led me to a room where we did all the usual first-time visit questions.

Because I tend to be sentimental, I must say that at this point I was struggling internally. Both Reese and Isaac were born at the same hospital in South Bend where I was born. I was greatly longing for the comforts of home in this pregnancy for many reasons. But I wanted this baby so much and was so impressed by God that the time was now that I was determined to make it through the awkwardness of a new doctor, new office, and new hospital.

These were the thoughts running through my mind as I nervously awaited meeting my new doctor. I can't remember what she looked like, and I do not even remember her name.

I do remember her coldness.

I do remember her looking at my chart and commenting on the births of my other children.

I do remember her looking at me and stating, "That is much too close together. Would you like me to do something about this?"

I do remember being stunned. Confused. Speechless.

I do remember finally breathing out a fierce, "No."

Did my new doctor, whom I just met, offer to abort my baby for me? Is that even allowed? I had never been treated this way or offered such a scenario by a medical professional.

Why did I stay?

Because it was just a means to an end.

Because my only other option was a much further drive and I had two young kids to think of being dragged all over for appointments.

Because, quite frankly, I didn't know what else to do.

Although I could hardly allow myself to breathe the words, I told one friend my experience several days later. She was horrified. I

Bowed Down to the Dust

made only the most necessary appointments from that time on and kept our interactions very brief.

A couple of months later I had to update a form for Medicaid. It had something to do with my being added on after Reese and Isaac. I am an educated woman. My degree is in English literature. And yet I could not figure out the way I should answer a certain question on this form. Looking back, I probably made it into something bigger than it needed to be. I probably could have just checked a box and been done with it. But I am also a big rule follower. I wanted to do this right and make sure that this whole process would be as seamless as possible; and I could get in and out with my new little baby, leaving all this government-regulated world behind me.

There was a phone number on the form. I started to call it in hopes that I could speak to someone and ask him or her my question. Every single time I called, the line was busy. I was beginning to get nervous on how to handle the situation.

After talking it over, Ben agreed to take a personal day from work and drive me to the Medicaid office about an hour away. We thought I could ask my question and then turn in the form in person. That would be even better than mailing it we surmised. A friend volunteered to watch Reese and Isaac for us, and we drove to the office to take care of business.

The minute we pulled up, I knew we had made a mistake. This was not the friendly WIC office with all of my kind nutritionists. A line snaked out the door, and the people were *mean*. After taking a number and waiting quite some time, I was finally called forward where I was berated for coming on a day that my caseworker was not in.

We tried to explain that I had absolutely no idea who my caseworker was or how to even find that information. Furthermore, every single time I called this place, which was numerous, the line was busy.

The person half-heartedly shrugged and told me to follow him behind the desk while Ben stayed behind in the waiting room. I turned the corner and entered a room where my heart immediately

Bowed Down to the Dust

sunk even further. The large room was lined with many cubicles. 20? 40? 50? And on every single cubicle, on the desks, on the chairs, on the floors, on the filing cabinets, were stacks upon stacks of papers. I glanced down at the little paper in my hand, with the one little question on the bottom that needed filling out; and I felt so small and so foolish.

The man sat me down and hurriedly answered my question. He told me what to write, took the form, stamped it, and set it down on the towering stack on his desk before rudely telling me not to come back again.

I left with a sick feeling that this would not end well.

A month later I received a form in the mail stating that my Medicaid had expired because they had not received the form from me. "I'll deal with this later," I thought, "I have my glucose test at the doctor's this afternoon."

I drove to the appointment and walked inside. The woman looked up my file and said, "I'm sorry. We can't see you anymore. Your Medicaid has expired."

"No, I turned in the form in person," I explained. "This is just some sort of mistake."

"I'm sorry," she said, "There is nothing we can do about it until this is fixed."

I left the office stunned. When Ben arrived home, late that night from working a 16-hour shift, he said he would take care of it. "Just call tomorrow and reschedule the test. We will pull the cash together to pay out of pocket for the test and the visit, and we'll keep doing that until this gets sorted out."

I called the next morning attempting to do just that. I was then informed that because I had been a Medicaid-patient they were legally prohibited from accepting any cash payments. I could not be seen until my Medicaid was reinstated.

I was happily married to a very hardworking man. I was a college graduate, former municipal employee and now the mother of two children with a third on the way. We had paid all of our taxes on time, every year. I was ready to have the all-important glucose test to

Bowed Down to the Dust

monitor both my health and the health of my unborn child; and I was completely shut out, turned away, and scorned by American medicine. I had no access. They would not even take the cash from my hand.

Jesus surely became to me the man of sorrows acquainted with *my* grief. Never had I identified with Him more as I was despised and rejected and man esteemed me not. If Jesus was not my closest friend before this, he surely became my closest friend then.

I began to make phone calls. I spent hours upon hours on the phone. I would leave messages only to call back a few days later because no one ever returned them. I checked my online account daily to see if anything had changed. We prayed. Our close friends were praying. After I spoke to one kind man at the state level several times, he finally offered me a number to call and then advised, "Sweetheart, you are going to have to be mean."

I waited until naptime. I waited until I was sure Reese and Isaac were both asleep because I was not proud of what I was about to do. I called the number. It, of course, went to voicemail. I left a message. And *I was mean*. I did not swear. I did not namecall. But I did yell. I did lament. I screamed about dropping the form off in person. I snarled that my doctor would not even allow me to pay for appointments. I demanded that they reinstate the benefits immediately so that I could get the tests I needed. I calmed down. I said, "Thank you," and hung up.

The next morning, I checked the online account again, and there it was—Medicaid reinstated. Jesus was afflicted on our account, and yet he opened not his mouth. I am not Jesus, and, sadly, I obviously *had* to open my mouth.

After nine months of this government-regulated emotional roller coaster, Raegan Lenee Hurt was born on March 15, 2011. She was a stunningly beautiful baby. Although I detected the doctor for a brief moment while I was pushing, the nurses thankfully did most of the caring for us. We had wanted to be surprised by her gender, both secretly hoping for another girl; and her daddy breathlessly cheered, "It's a little girl," upon her arrival.

Bowed Down to the Dust

 Throughout our hospital stay, we kept staring down at our precious baby girl and commenting on how happy we were to have her. Elated would have been the more appropriate word. She made all of our hearts swoon, including that little baby boy who was "too close in age to her."

 When Ben and the kids came to pick me up from the hospital to go home, I was holding Raegan in my arms. The nurse walked in and took her from me to cut her little bracelets off. Isaac lost it. Reaching out for her, he started screaming, "baby, baby, baby!" We could immediately sense his fear and started trying to calm him, "No, Isaac, it's ok, the baby is coming home with us." But he cried all the way down the hall, creating quite a scene while screaming for his baby sister. He did not stop crying until her car seat was safely buckled in the car next to him and he could reach over and hold her tiny hand.

 We pulled out of the hospital parking lot with our three children, finally saying goodbye to the doctor who offered to abort the littlest one among us. Isaac, close to babyhood himself, held her small hand all the way home.

Bowed Down to the Dust

Reese and Isaac meeting their baby sister for the first time; look how smitten he is!

Bowed Down to the Dust

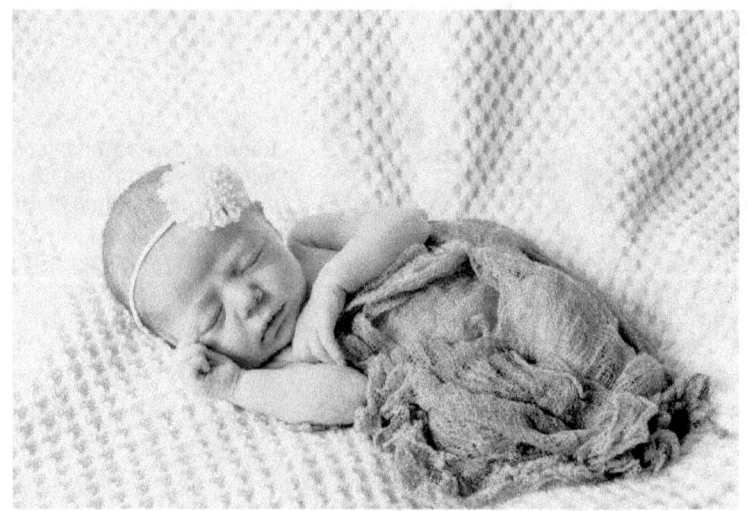

Our beautiful Raegan Lenee—a gift from God.

Bowed Down to the Dust

A Broken-down Car, A Prayer, and an Envelope

When Ben and I married, we both had fairly new cars. We took good care of them, keeping up on the maintenance and paying both of them off before Reese was born. In fact, paying off Ben's Ford Focus was the last thing we had to do in order for me to be able to stay home with her.

It was that same silver Ford Focus that suddenly began wildly shaking as we crossed the street from Aldi to our apartment complex. But we weren't simply crossing the street. This was Ogden Avenue with 5 lanes of heavy traffic! I was pregnant with Raegan, and I had Reese and Isaac with me too. I began praying loudly and boldly over this vehicle, "Lord God, do not allow this car to die on this road right now! Holy Spirit, become the power that brings this engine back to life!" I was keenly aware that my husband, on any given day, could be within a two hour radius of us with his job. I simply did not know what I would do if our car died in the middle of that road with my children inside of it.

The Lord answered that prayer. We pulled the shaking and lurching car into the apartment parking lot where it completely died as soon as I left the road. I coasted into the nearest parking spot. Reese, 4 years old at the time, jumped up and exclaimed, "It's okay,

Bowed Down to the Dust

Mommy. If Jesus wants us to have a broken-down car, we will just say, 'Thank you, Jesus, for this broken-down car.'" I love that child.

Ben had a friend over to look at it for us that weekend. He delivered the awful news: cracked engine block. To this day we have no idea how that happened. We took good care of that car. It was only nine years old, and it hadn't been in any kind of accidents. I guess Jesus truly did just want us to have a broken-down car.

Our hands were literally tied. We had no cash to buy a cheap used car; we had burned through our savings the year before when we were paying rent and groceries. We truly could not afford even a small car payment and didn't think it would be wise to take on debt at that time. We hadn't had a car payment in nearly five years. We prayed the prayer of the Israelites, "We do not know what to do, Lord, but our eyes are on you."

I recalled one of our first weeks in Illinois when my beautiful friend, Kimberly, invited the kids and me over for lunch. "Do you have two cars?" she sweetly asked. She was inquiring to make sure it wouldn't be a hindrance for me to get to their house in Wheaton during the day while Ben was working.

"Yes, we have two cars." I replied, my heart twisting into knots. "Not having two cars," I thought, "I couldn't survive that." Well, here we were. I was about to have to survive that.

My car was still running well, but it was about to add to our predicament. Our little Raegan was growing inside my womb and would eventually need out, but my car was a 2 door, 4 seatbelt Escort. Anyone can do the math and know that something had to give.

Every night, and many times throughout the day too, we brought our needs before the Lord. We were convinced that He had tied our hands in this because He was going to reveal Himself in a big way. We just weren't sure when or what it would look like.

We started to have people ask us, "What are you guys doing about a car?"

"We are just praying about it," we would say. Truly, there was nothing else we *could* say.

Bowed Down to the Dust

Ben worked with a guy named Rob who took a big interest in our situation and would regularly ask him what the vehicle status was. Ben would share honestly that we were trusting for the Lord to provide somehow. Ben's supervisor would sometimes let him take a company car home, something that the other technicians never did. It gave us a bit more flexibility. I wouldn't have to take him to work every morning, and it allowed me to have a car during the day sometimes. We were so grateful, but that situation ended when the owner became aware of the situation. We certainly understood. They shouldn't show us special treatment.

We continued praying for three months. We adjusted to juggling life and sharing one car. I repented of my pride, and the Lord brought me to a place where it really didn't bother me anymore. Except for the fact that Raegan kept growing and in a few more months we wouldn't be able to fit our whole family in the Escort anymore.

In our three months of praying, we were also specifically asking the Lord to provide a minivan and asking if He would be so kind to do so before Christmas. Those are specific requests, but we had reasons for them. Our kids are very spoiled by their grandparents; and the previous year my parents had to drive the two hours one way, following us home after Christmas because we couldn't fit the kids, our suitcases, and their gifts in our car at the same time! We were hoping to alleviate a trip for them. (We also regularly asked our parents not to get the kids so many things, but they never listened, much to our children's delight.)

A few days before Christmas, Ben called while I was washing dishes at the kitchen sink.

"Someone called me today," he said.

"Yes..." I responded.

"They've known that we have been praying for the Lord to provide us a car, and they want to give us theirs!"

"What!" I exclaimed, as I dropped a bowl into the sudsy water.

"And there's more. It's a van. And it will be ready for us on Saturday to drive home for Christmas." Ben's joy was discernible on the other end of the phone line as my own tears of joy rolled down

Bowed Down to the Dust

my cheeks. To say that we were rejoicing and praising God was an understatement. After hanging up with me, Ben got the privilege of finding Rob in the shop to tell him, "The Lord provided a van for us today!"

Rob's mouth fell open wide, and he said, "I have to admit when you told me you were trusting God to provide, I thought you were crazy. I've never heard anything like this."

Ben had shared the Gospel with Rob several months before during a combined late-night job. It is a humbling memory for him as he had to leave a softball game he was about to play with some guys from church, and he was furious to receive a call for work. His anger was intense, and he yelled all the way to the job. But when he arrived and Rob started asking multiple questions about Jesus, he was humbled to see that the Lord had a bigger plan that day, worth so much more than a softball game. We don't know if Rob ever came to see his need for Jesus, but we do know that he has heard the truth and has seen God work in the lives of needy, broken people, namely us.

We took the kids on Saturday to pick up our new van. We profusely thanked the givers of this gift. They wanted to be anonymous and asked us not to tell anyone that they had given it. We were blown away by it! It was perfect for our growing family. Singing worship songs through our tears, we drove it home for Christmas. In the middle of the highway I opened up the glove box. Inside was an envelope titled, "For you." I opened it and exclaimed, "I can't take it anymore!" Peeking out of the envelope were three crisp $100 bills!

The Lord didn't have to do any of that. We were learning to praise Him regardless of the circumstances. And the owners of that van, special friends to this day, certainly did not have to give us either of those gifts. The Lord does amazing things both when we wait on Him and when we are willing to be used by Him.

A Dreaded Call, A Broken Tent, and Special Balloons

On February 15, 2011 my phone rang. It was my sister-in-law, Carol, married to Ben's oldest brother Steve.

"Nikki," she said, "Steve and Doris (Ben's parents) are at Josh's house. They had to call the ambulance...It doesn't look good. You guys need to pray."

"Oh no," I said, "Let me go get Ben. Are they taking him to the hospital?"

"No, you don't understand. It's too late."

I think the words were just too difficult for any of us to say. Ben's older brother, the second born Hurt son, had passed away unexpectedly at 34 years old. He was sitting in a chair with his coat and shoes on. His mother, my precious mother-in-law, had found her own son, lifelessly waiting for her by the door.

The next few hours were a flurry of activity. I remember Ben hitting his knees in anguish and confusion after more phone calls came from his Dad and Stevie. There were phone calls with both of our families, our small group, and our pastors. We had just laid our kids down for bed, and we would need to pack for a trip and drive the two hours home.

"What do you need me to do? Do you need to go home right now?" I asked him. "I will start packing right away."

Bowed Down to the Dust

In the end, we allowed the kids a full night's sleep before we headed home to continue grieving with the family. Ben was not as close to his brother in adulthood as he would have liked. But, nevertheless, he was devastated to have lost him at this point in their lives. And our hearts were completely crushed for his wonderful parents who now carried the burden of burying a son.

We were loading the car up to leave the next morning when we realized we had a flat tire. Completely overwhelmed at the dark days ahead of us, we were knocked down by this seemingly trivial task. When one of our pastors called to check on us and see if we needed anything, we told him about the tire. He came immediately to take care of it for us.

I drove us all the way home. Reese, almost five, started asking many questions. I tried to help Ben answer her as best I could. He lovingly explained to her that our bodies are like tents. Our real person, our soul, just lives inside the tent. A few moments later he erupted into tears. It scared Isaac, who was not quite 2-years-old; and he started to cry too. Reese leaned over to her baby brother and said, "It's okay Isaac. Daddy is just sad because Uncle Josh's tent is broken."

We made it home in record time. Although Ben's company had nothing close to this in their employee handbook, they offered him an entire week of paid leave. This gesture went a long way, and we were so grateful not to have to rush back to Illinois while the rest of the family was together.

We stayed at Steve and Carol's house and slept in our niece's room. I recall waking up the morning of the funeral with our arms held tight to each other with Reese, Isaac, and even Raegan, almost ready to be born, in between us. We were both sobbing. I couldn't shake the feeling that once upon a time my in-laws had most likely laid in their own bed with Stevie, Josh, Ben, and Joe all in between them. I saw them in my mind's eye and knew that they were happy then. All six Hurts safe and together, never knowing that one day they would need to say goodbye so soon to one of them.

Bowed Down to the Dust

We had dinner at the church after the burial. My other sister-in-law, Adrianne, had the idea of all the nieces and nephews writing notes on balloons and releasing them to say goodbye to their Uncle Josh. Outside, we were able to smile through tears as the kids waved and cheerfully yelled, "Goodbye, Uncle Josh!" "We love you."

Five years later, and again in February, the Hurt family phone lines were once again buzzing, "The twins are here!" The Lord turned our sorrow into rejoicing. Ben's parents, Grandma D. and Grandpa Steve, were blessed with their last grandchildren: Harper Jean, named after her maternal Great-Grandmother and Hudson Joshua, named after the uncle, brother, and son who left us too soon.

*Uncle Josh with our nephew, Israel.
He is truly missed!*

Bowed Down to the Dust

Daddy singing to Hudson Joshua and Harper Jean, born in 2016.

Bowed Down to the Dust

My heart swoons; I am so delighted they are all mine!

Bowed Down to the Dust

Bowed Down to the Dust

Our completed family of seven at Notre Dame in 2017.

Bowed Down to the Dust

The East and West Wings of California Avenue

Raegan was three months old when we closed the door for the last time at the apartment on Landing Drive and opened the door on California Avenue, moving in with a family from our church, the Segers. *You moved in with a family from your church?* Yes, we did! They had offered 3 times before. If I knew what a blessing it would become, they would have only asked once.

While pregnant with Raegan, Ben made a pact with me that if things didn't change with his position at work by the time she was born then we would look to move out of Illinois. If nothing else, it was sure to give our family a better standard of living. (We had a number of families in our church from the east coast. More than once, one of them told me that they had moved to the Chicago area for a better standard of living! They obviously hadn't heard of Indiana!)

Part of our dilemma was that Ben's company kept holding out a promise of a better salaried position for him. They were planning to create a leadership role for him, complete with higher pay, no on-call time, and a company car. The problem was this had been talked about for many months with no endgame in sight.

The Segers were a young couple and newer to our small group. Jonathan was an engineer for Caterpillar; and Misha stayed home with their little boy, Davin, who was nine months younger than Isaac.

Bowed Down to the Dust

They had just bought their first home. It had four bedrooms at the top of their stairs, but they were only using two. We turned them down the first couple of times that they offered; and I would say to Ben, "They know we have three kids, right?"

I finally agreed after their third offer because I sincerely thought we would be there for two weeks. Harkening back to his promise, Ben had contacted a restoration company in South Bend to inquire about a job. By this time, he had several different certifications in the carpet cleaning/water restoration world and had some marketable skills to offer. Our lease was about to expire at the apartment, and we didn't want to be locked into another one when we were considering moving again. So, this time, we took the Segers up on their offer. We put most of our things into a storage unit and set off for their beautiful brick two story home on California Avenue on the opposite end of Aurora.

The Segers had the "west wing" for themselves, and they cleared out the whole "east wing" at the top of the stairs for us. Ben and I shared the room with Raegan while Reese and Isaac shared the other room next to us. Misha and I set about creating a meal schedule. We didn't have a set schedule for the weekends, but during the week she and I took turns cooking for the whole crew. We set up laundry schedules too, switching off and on for which family would use the washing machine each day.

This young family threw open their doors and rolled out the carpet for a *loud* family of five. Early on Misha had bought some new things for the house and asked *me* where *I* wanted to put them. I remember feeling so puzzled and laughed saying, "You don't have to ask me. It's your house."

She replied sweetly, "Well, no, it's your house now too."

Much to my surprise, those two weeks turned into nine months. Ben was offered the job in South Bend; but after much prayer and soul searching, we did not sense a release in leaving Illinois quite yet. His company kept promising that they would create this position for him, and we decided to wait and see how things unfolded with his current employer.

Bowed Down to the Dust

So, we settled into life at the Seger's. Our boys quickly became like brothers, a relationship they continue to share to this day. One night I lay Isaac down for bed in his crib. Later on, Misha came upstairs to put Davin to bed; he was abnormally struggling that night to go to sleep. After listening to Davin cry for several minutes from his crib down the hall, Isaac yelled out, "Davin! Go to sleep!" Davin quickly settled down.

Another evening, Misha and Jonathan invited some friends from our church to join us for dinner. We all crammed into the dining room and sat around the table eating tacos and enjoying the company. Isaac, who was used to watching a show on my laptop at the table when it was my turn to make dinner, looked around at all the fixings and muttered under his breath, "Aww, man, now I can't watch my movie. There's taco everywhere." Life was certainly not dull when our two families shared a home.

Now that we were committed to sticking it out in Illinois; we began to search for a home of our own. We had actually been searching for a house to buy ever since we landed in Illinois. Aside from the maintenance costs that a home can bring, a monthly payment on a mortgage could have proven to be much less than we were paying to rent. We hoped that by purchasing a home we could both lower our monthly expenses while also allowing us the opportunity to feel a little more settled in our community. There is not much community to be had in an apartment complex with its high turnover of tenants.

The Segers assured us that they had no timeline on our stay with them. They were open to us remaining with them for however long the Lord had ordained. Their sweet hospitality afforded us the time to house hunt. We found a tri-level with a unique floorplan in a cute little neighborhood on the west side of Aurora, near to another young family from our church and still close to our housemates whom we couldn't imagine moving far away from. It was being offered as a short-sale, and many of our friends had been quite successful at purchasing short sale homes post the 2009 housing crash. If you had the luxury of putting in a little wait time for one, it could end up

Bowed Down to the Dust

being a major blessing. We prayerfully put in an offer on the tri-level and were ecstatic when it was accepted!

We were finally able to turn the corner from constantly asking, "What are we doing? Why are we here?" Ben still desired to be in ministry; it was a constant prayer that we offered before the Lord. However, we also felt our family needed to put down some roots and stop being so transient.

We continued to delight in our time with the Segers, knowing it was a special and unique time in our lives, while we waited for all the paperwork on the house to come through. I remember one particular conversation with Misha. I am the youngest of three girls in my family. Misha is the oldest of two girls. One day I confessed to her, "Misha, even though I am several years older than you. I always feel like I am talking to my older sisters. I think that's why I feel so safe with you."

She laughed and said, "I know exactly what you mean! I always feel like I am talking to my younger sister when I am with you." And that is truly and most likely the secret to our friendship and our ability to join our two families together for so long. I am used to being a bit coddled, and she is used to mothering. She took care of me, and I looked up to her.

Although we were definitely blessed with an amazing friendship and a special living arrangement, there were still times of intense struggle in my heart. Many days it seemed Jonathan saw more of my kids than their own father did. I am eternally grateful for all the times "Laugher Paffer" (Reese's nickname for Jonathan) wrestled with and threw balls with my kids in the backyard or watched *Pinky and the Brain* with them in the basement while I completed a chore. But still, I was jealous for their own dad to have all those experiences with them. And as much as I felt at home with the Segers, I also wanted to make sure that we never took advantage of their benevolence. This meant that I cleaned every cereal bowl immediately, not wanting to leave a hint of a mess in our wake; and I sought to keep Reese, Isaac, and Raegan within my ear shot at all moments of the

Bowed Down to the Dust

day. I collapsed into bed exhausted most nights, oftentimes still waiting for Ben to clock out for the day.

As the months rolled along, word on the short sale grew scarce. Finally, shortly before Raegan's first birthday, we received some dreaded news. The owners, who were still living in the home, had completely stopped communicating with the bank. Not only that, but it came to our attention after all those months of waiting on progress that the home had three liens on it. That meant three different banks needed to be communicated with, and all of them had to agree on the settlement together. We had arrived at a stalemate. We had to walk away; our short sale was not meant to be.

Several months later the house went on the market as a foreclosure. I called our realtor, and we jetted over to see it. Listed for mere pennies, I was tentatively hopeful. We would have been able to purchase it for significantly less than even our short-sale agreement. Our realtor warned me, however, that it may not be in the best condition. He was right. The occupants had torn huge holes through most of the drywall throughout the home and bent, twisted, and stole piping. The repairs were beyond our pocketbook and our expertise.

As the short sale fell through, another family in our church alerted us to a home on their street that was going up as a rental soon. The Segers had kept us safely in the womb of their home for nine months, but it was time to be reborn as an independent family unit! We told Jonathan and Misha the news; we had found a nearby rental property and would be moving out that month. They informed us that another Baby Seger would soon be occupying one of the rooms in the Hurt Wing. The timing was perfect.

Bowed Down to the Dust

Reese and Isaac, enjoying donuts in the Seger's kitchen on California Avenue.

Reese, Isaac, Davin, and Jonathan playing games in the living room. Notice Ben, having just arrived home, eating a late dinner in the kitchen.

Bowed Down to the Dust

Misha, feeling accomplished in the kitchen!

*Reese, Raegan, Isaac, and Davin—
all together in the wagon on the driveway!*

Bowed Down to the Dust

Buzz and Woody—Brothers for life!

Bowed Down to the Dust

New York Street, Knocks at the Door, and a Pile of Rocks

The day after we moved into the rental on New York Street, a police officer knocked on our door. "Hello, we're canvassing the neighborhood to see if you saw anything related to the robbery at the beginning of the week."

"The robbery!" I exclaimed, "No, we just moved in."

The officer paused, looked around, leaned forward and said, "This street has been robbed 3 times in the last year. Get a dog."

What an introduction to New York Street! Our friends, the Underhills, who lived across the street and a few doors down, had lived on the street for several years and had not experienced any problems. We trusted them and prayed for the Lord's protection to be over our home. I honestly never struggled or lived in fear. There were annoying things about it, like the eyesore of the horribly chipping red paint on the exterior of the home. An ordinance worker from the city came to do a check on the home a few months after we moved in, and the owners were flagged and made to paint the exterior of the home as well as modify some of the interior. I had some interesting experiences while living there for sure, but nothing that made me feel our lives were in danger. We never did get a dog.

One hilarious encounter occurred one evening while Ben was at work. I had just finished giving Isaac a bath when I heard a knock on

Bowed Down to the Dust

the door. I opened the door to the smiling faces of a black man and two black women. "Hello," they said, "We are from the small church at the end of the street, and we would love to know how we can pray for you." At that precise moment, Raegan pinched her fingers in the door and started wailing, Reese started calling me from the kitchen, and Isaac streaked into the living room stark naked to see what the commotion was all about. Overwhelmed with the moment, I hurriedly thanked them, asked them to pray for my children and me, and politely closed the door so that my son wouldn't continue exposing himself to the strangers.

I tended to Raegan's hurt fingers, dressed Isaac in his pajamas, and went to find out what Reese needed in the kitchen. Once things calmed, I looked across the street and saw our friends, the Underhills, relaxing on their front porch, fellowshipping and praying with these fellow believers that had first come to my house. I was desperate for company and jealous of the time they were getting to share as I walked Raegan upstairs for bedtime and checked the clock to see how much longer until Ben came home. I also prayed, "Lord, please let me have another chance to talk and pray with these people."

Several weeks later, there was another knock on the door, and again I found three smiling faces looking up at me. My children were contentedly watching a cartoon in the basement, so I enthusiastically greeted my guests, "Hello! I'm so happy you came back!" I exclaimed. Met with somewhat quizzical looks, one of the women tentatively said, "Well...hello...but I don't think we've met before."

"You came a few weeks ago to pray with me, but then my son ran naked into the room, and I didn't get a chance to talk to you," I reminded them.

My front door guests laughed and corrected me. They had not been to my house before. They *were* from a church, but *not* the church down the street, they were Jehovah Witnesses. I doubt they were used to such an enthusiastic welcome from a homeowner. I chuckled inside at my mistake and apologized for the confusion. I

Bowed Down to the Dust

took the literature they offered and closed the door again, still wishing for the sweet prayer time with the first group of like-minded believers.

Our most interesting experiences, though, while living on New York Street came through our next-door neighbor, Mae. Mae lived alone and talked to no one. She, another renter, lived in the original converted carriage house for the street during the days of horses and buggies. Sarah, my friend across the street, told me at one point that Mae's home was actually on a list of buildings waiting to be condemned by the city. This was no surprise as it was tiny and decrepit, looking as if it could implode any moment.

I've always loved being friendly with my neighbors. But Mae made it impossible. Anytime I would see her and start to say hello she would literally run behind her front door. I would catch her at times having a quiet conversation with Reese who was coloring on the porch. "Hello, Mae," Reese would say.

"Well, hi there," Mae would reply.

I would begin to walk out, to say hello myself; and the moment she heard the door open, off she'd go.

Our bedroom was on the main floor at the front of the house. I have always been a sound sleeper, but one morning I woke up around 5:00 am to a constant thud hitting the side of the house. I woke Ben up and he groggily said, "Oh, that's just Mae."

"What do you mean?" I asked, a little frightened.

"I didn't want to scare you, but she has some sort of routine that she does early in the morning," he replied.

"Huh... and what is that sound?"

"Go peek behind the blinds and see for yourself." he replied as he yawned.

I padded across the hardwood floors and peeked through the blinds on the side window. Sure enough, there was Mae illuminated by the light of the streetlamp, throwing small rocks at the side of our house.

"What is she doing?!" I whispered to Ben through clenched teeth.

Bowed Down to the Dust

He just shook his head slowly and said, "I have no idea. But she does this routine every morning. You've just always slept through it."

I continued to watch as she kept slinging the rocks for several seconds. Then she walked back to her front door where she had a coffee mug sitting on a window ledge. She took a sip of coffee, set the mug down, and grabbed two small 5 lb. weights. She started pacing back and forth on her gravel drive; and as she neared the street, she slammed her two weights together. When she finished these repetitions, she walked back over to the window ledge, put the weights down, took another sip of coffee, and walked back over to face our house with another pile of rocks.

Thus began early mornings with our neighbor, Mae.

Several weeks later Ben and the kids were tossing a ball around in the backyard. Isaac accidentally kicked it over the fence into Mae's yard. Ben walked into the house to tell me what had happened, "Don't look at me," I laughed, "but take Reese with you to get it. She likes her."

I could not resist the temptation to spy on them as they met with Mae. I ran to our side bedroom window and peeked through the blinds again while Ben, who took all the kids as our hopeful peace offerings, strolled over and knocked on her front door. I couldn't see her face at all, but I saw the door open and our kids smile. They stood talking for a few moments, and then I watched them all walk to the back of the house together to retrieve our kickball.

I left the window and went to the front porch to meet them. My chuckling ended when I saw Ben's face. He looked contemplative and forlorn. "What happened?" I asked him.

He waited until the kids were out of earshot and responded, "She opened the door but refused to look me in the eye. I told her we had kicked a ball behind her house and asked if we could go back there to get it. She just kept shuffling her feet around and saying, 'Yes, sir' over and over."

He continued, "The thought dropped into my mind that this is perhaps a woman who has been wounded by many men."

Bowed Down to the Dust

The thought sat heavy upon both of our hearts. Ben, near to tears, grabbed my hand as we walked back to the yard to continue playing with the kids.

A handful of times Mae got into her rock throwing routine during the day. However, that wasn't her preferred MO. She favored the early-morning, 5:00 am sessions. A neighbor once called the cops on her during one of her daytime escapades. We watched as three police cars pulled onto the street and approached her in her gravel drive. She shuffled her feet and looked down at them while they spoke with her too.

We never called the cops on Mae for anything. Her sessions grew to be both our morning alarm clock and a gentle reminder from a loving Father to pray for the quiet, and most likely tortured, woman who lived next door.

First day on New York Street!

Bowed Down to the Dust

*Reese and Isaac playing outside.
Notice Mae's roofline behind the fence.*

Bowed Down to the Dust

A Cloud of Despair, a Tough Conversation, and a New Opportunity

By living with the Segers for nine months, we were able to add to a savings account for the first time since moving to Illinois. But as soon as we moved out, we started bleeding income once again. Ben's job was just not meant to be something that an entire family could depend on, at least not in that state with its incredibly high housing costs. We've bought two different houses in Indiana since renting the house on New York Street, and neither one of those mortgages have come anywhere near to what we had to pay to live on that street in Illinois. Not only that, but both of the houses we bought were in better condition and not on streets that had been robbed several times in a short manner of time.

We began to see our savings dwindle every month throughout the late spring and summer. We were once again dependent on those saved dollars to provide for basic necessities. I began to ask Ben the dreaded question, "What are we doing? We can't sustain living here." This changed in the fall. Ben's hours and on-call assignments increased significantly. He was able, through all of the overtime, to provide a sustainable living wage; but we then had the opposite side of the problem. The kids and I never saw him. He was working 80-100 hours *every* week. I was beginning to experience low level depression, which carried with it a cloud of despair that hung over

Bowed Down to the Dust

me. As much as I loved being with my three children every day and was grateful for how hard my husband worked to accomplish that, I just longed to be in the same room with him. And Reese, nearly 7-years-old, was old enough to express her sadness over missing Daddy too.

The days would consistently look like this:

Ben would call midway through the day and say, "I think I should be home by 6:00 tonight; my list is shorter today! We can have dinner together."

An hour later I'd receive another call, "Well, they added a couple jobs to me, but they took one off that was farther away. I think I can still make it by 6:30. Try to hold the kids off from eating if you can."

Then, "I'm sorry...a call just came in. I am the closest to it. I need to go quote this job. I won't make it home before 8:00. Go ahead and eat without me. Tell the kids that I love them."

Finally, "I'm on my way back to the shop. I have to drop these dehumidifiers off inside, and then I'll come home. It will be close to 10:00. I'm sorry. Did the kids go to bed ok?"

At this time our church finally had a need for another small group leader. We had waited over three years to have some sort of leadership role in which to pour ourselves. Our pastors asked Ben if he would consider leading this new group, and we quickly surmised that it was basically impossible. His work schedule would never allow it. On top of that, our time together as a family was nearly extinct.

Oh, the irony! We left everything and moved to this place to become a part of this church, and now we could not even serve the church that we came here for. Our friend, Erin, used to say, "The Hurts not only put all their eggs into one basket, but they picked up the basket and moved it to Illinois." We sadly explained our dilemma to our pastors and turned what we considered to be a great privilege down.

Around this time, Ben and I hit a climatic tipping point in our relationship. I confessed, one late night through many tears, that I felt he loved the church more than he loved me. *Ouch.*

Bowed Down to the Dust

    Ben had, even with all the crazy work responsibilities, developed deep friendships and accountability with the men in our church. They encouraged him greatly through all of our trials. He was able to be vulnerable, maybe for the first time in his life, with other believers. He had fun with these men but could also have deep theological discussions with them. He had many opportunities to be involved in different men's groups throughout our years there. These usually met early on Saturday mornings. I was happy for him to be a part, remembering that we moved there *for the church;* and I wanted him to be blessed for working so hard. But it was also challenging to be left alone again while he involved himself in these ministries.

    Scripture is clear that we should love the church, which is Christ's body here on earth; but husbands are actually called to love their wives as Christ loved the church, which means laying down his life for her. I needed to confess it seemed he was willing to lay down his life for the church but not necessarily for me. After I finally shared this inner turmoil with Ben, he listened. I think the Lord used it to start a change in his heart. The bonds that were so strong to these people began to loosen as he began to clearly see what our life there was doing to his family. Although a tough conversation, it was one that we needed to have. It started to turn our affections in a different way. Ben wanted to show *by his actions* that I was more important to him than the church. We began to pray that the Lord would open another door for our family, one that would ensure he could be with his family more.

    This all led to Ben again calling the restoration company in South Bend that had extended him an offer 18 months before. They informed him that they were not planning to hire at the time but invited him to come back in for another interview anyway. This company has been around the South Bend area for many years. We knew that they ran their business much differently than the company in Illinois. They may not have offered the mandatory rest times that I grew up seeing my dad receive, but they definitely sought to give their guys more regular hours that wouldn't interfere with family life quite as much. (Fast forward several months at this new company

Bowed Down to the Dust

when Ben worked an incredible amount of overtime during a huge polar vortex that fell upon South Bend in the winter of 2011. The company sent me a huge bouquet of flowers. The card attached read, "Thank you for sharing so much of your husband during these unprecedented times." A seemingly small gesture, but still soothing for my soul after all the long emergency hours we experienced in Illinois.)

Ben would still be on call; it is the nature of the water restoration business. But we wouldn't have to expect the extreme ups and downs like we had endured the past 3 1/2 years. And just living in Indiana alone would feel like getting a raise due to the change in cost of living. We drove through a blizzard to get to the interview. They offered him a job on the spot. Apparently, they were hiring! He willingly accepted it without even discussing it with me. The only obstacle remaining was finding a place to live and figuring out where our family of five would attend church.

My love. We've had 18 years years of tough conversations between us.

Bowed Down to the Dust

Going Back, Moving Forward

"When are you due with your baby?" the sweet, petite woman asked me.

"In May," I told her. "It's our second baby."

"Oh, congratulations!" she exclaimed.

It was the spring of 2009, and I had been invited by a friend to a live Nancy-Leigh DeMoss taping with Revive our Hearts. I sat in the room with many women, listening to this woman of God dissect God's Word. At one point, during a break, this same petite woman, who shared her name was Andrea, stood up and gave a testimony about planting a church in Granger with her husband. "I would never plant a church," I thought. But for some reason, meeting her and hearing of this new little church plant stuck in my mind. Just a few months later while I was holding my baby boy, Ben came home and said he was confident the Lord was leading us to move away.

After our tough conversation in the fall of 2012, we began to listen to some online preaching by a man, Trent Griffith, out of a church in Granger, Indiana. We liked what we were hearing. He understood that the Gospel has something to say about our lives *every single day*. It's not just what we need for salvation. We don't receive it one time and then move on to greater truths. It *IS* the greatest truth, and its applications are *the* source of joy for Christ followers.

Bowed Down to the Dust

"Ben, I'm confident this is the husband of that woman I met at the Nancy Leigh DeMoss event a few years ago," I said one morning after listening to a sermon. We both agreed that if the Lord led us back to the South Bend area this church would most likely be a good fit for our family.

After accepting the job in South Bend a few months later, we began to realize how many reasons we had to rejoice. We would be living, once again, in greater proximity to both of our families. Our kids would grow up with weekly, maybe even daily, interactions with their grandparents and the cousins, aunts and uncles that were so dear to us all. I could still hear Reese stamping her foot in one of the many homes we tried to buy in Illinois and saying, "No! This is not close to my cousins!" Or the time we went to dinner with Ben's family before we left for Illinois, and she reached across to hold her cousin Lyndi's hand and with a tear rolling down her 3-year-old cheek said, "But Lyndi, I am going to miss you so much." We were overjoyed to have the time to redeem all those family moments.

We also anticipated finally getting a break in our finances. It would be much easier to raise our three children in the great cornfields of Indiana replete with one of the lowest housing costs in the nation. Besides all of that, I just really love my hometown. I was never ashamed to be from South Bend and considered it a great place to live.

We had so much to rejoice over, but we also deeply mourned and wept. We moved to Illinois with a dream of getting plugged into this Gospel-centered church and hopefully being admitted to their pastor's college with the goal of pastoring in one of their churches. Many people along the way expressed their concern for our pursuit. But we couldn't ignore the pull that this path had on us. Nevertheless, it was a dream that was never realized. And for a man who picked up his basket and set it down in a different town with an entire family depending on him, that was not an easy dream to let go of. Whispers of failure often dominated Ben's thoughts. He had to swallow his pride to come home as a carpet cleaner and not the pastor that he had hoped to be.

Bowed Down to the Dust

About a year after we moved to Illinois, our church did send two men and their families to Maryland to attend the pastor's college. These men were faithful servants of God and the church. They had been involved in the church for many years prior to our arrival. One of them was our small group leader, Josh Anderson and his wife Kimberly, whom we loved so much. We were so happy for them. They still faithfully serve Redeemer Community Church to this day. It was the right choice, as determined by the Lord.

Two weeks after we moved into the Seger's house and shortly before our friends left for the pastor's college, a torrent of upheaval was reported from within Sovereign Grace Ministries. We were completely out of touch with what was happening at the ministry headquarters in Maryland. All we knew and experienced was that our pastors feared the Lord and loved the people in our church. They have our utmost respect. Our church, after many months of prayer and counsel, ended up leaving Sovereign Grace Ministries, and Ben's dream of being sent to their pastor's college essentially ended. We clung to the truth, "It is better to take refuge in the Lord than to trust in man" (Psalm 118:8).

So, in leaving, we not only had to walk through the loss of that dream but also the loss of a family that was our Redeemer Church. It is a delightful thing to belong to the family of God. You have an instant connection with other Christ followers. Yes, we knew some better than others, but we loved them all as extended family. Many of them stood by us encouraging us, supporting us, praying for us, and at times even helping to provide for us. It was *painful* to say goodbye to our dear friends.

The Segers, our most treasured friends, wrote us a letter and gave it to us the week that we moved:

4/4/2013
Dear Ben, Nikki, Reese, Isaac, & Raegan,

This is a letter that we thought we would never have to write. (Okay, maybe that's not true... There were 2 or 3 times when we were sure

Bowed Down to the Dust

you were moving back home, then relieved that you were staying, then nervous that you were going back home, etc. Haha!) But we digress...

Having you & your family stay with us for nine months was one of the best decisions we, as a married couple, have ever made. Even though Ben ate all our treats, God was so kind & blessed us with a friendship that we'll cherish forever.

Here are some of the things we will never forget, in no particular order.
- *Jonathan & Ben's guitar & xylophone concert in the basement.*
- *Reese repeatedly calling Jonathan a "laugher paffer."*
- *Isaac coloring his entire body in marker.*
- *Reagan's random shouts and subsequent smiles after everyone looked at her.*
- *Sitting around a crowded table.*
- *Isaac flipping backwards in his chair.*
- *Misha & Nikki's heart-to-heart conversations throughout the day.*
- *Jonathan & Ben's gaseous explosions... all the time!*
- *Playing Dominion at night after the kids went to bed.*
- *Davin & Isaac acting like brothers... and the good, the bad, and the ugly that comes along with that.*
- *Jonathan & Ben throwing Reese, Isaac, & Davin around in the basement.*
- *Nikki talking to Misha behind her nursing cover, making her look like a ninja.*
- *The extra decibels that come along with the Hurt family.*
- *Stromboli's & cookies... Yum!*
- *Our lifelong friends, no matter where they live.*
- *Seeing God provide again and again and again.*

*But the thing we will remember the most from your time with us is a testimony of God's faithfulness. We got to experience secondhand the faithfulness of God in **your** lives. And He continues to remain*

Bowed Down to the Dust

faithful in this new venture of your lives. Though we would like God's faithfulness in your lives to be played out in Aurora, God works in mysterious and often not-as-we-would-prefer ways. (At least Ben's undying love for Notre Dame will not be so easily mocked since you'll be living so close to it!) God was faithful in the past, He is faithful now, and we are sure that He will continue to be faithful to you throughout the rest of your lives.

We love you dearly. You will be missed so much. And we'll be sure to text, call, and visit as often as we can.

With much love,
Jonathan, Misha, Davin, & Levi Seger

    We also needed to say goodbye to our dear small group. It had multiplied by this point, and we were meeting in two separate homes. The Andersons called the entire original group together, one last time, a couple weeks before we moved. It was good for my soul to be in the same room with all of those people together. My emotions overwhelmed me, though, and I could hardly speak. Ben shared some words, through his tears, and at one point said, "You guys did so well to draw out our hearts. There were nights that we were determined not to share anything because we didn't want to dominate the need to be cared for. We would show up for the group, and you would ask just the right question to get us talking; and before we knew it, our hearts were cared for and encouraged."

    Josh, with a smile, responded, "It wasn't hard to get you talking, Ben." The group echoed with much laughter.

    We loved this group. It was their ministry to us that prompted Ben to comment several times to me, "If I ever get to be in ministry again, I think I want it to be over small groups."

    Our families were told and were ecstatic with our decision. Our church was told and was encouraging us to walk by faith as always. Now it was time to look for housing! We had one good weekend to find our family a home before we needed to vacate the rental on New

Bowed Down to the Dust

York Street. We were easily approved for a mortgage because even though we had struggled so much financially over the past few years we never took on any debt and were able to stay within our means. We looked on the north side of South Bend and found the perfect tri-level in a family-friendly neighborhood just north of Notre Dame's campus on Tally-Ho Dr. It was 5 minutes from Ben's parents and only 20 minutes from mine. We knew the church we wanted to attend couldn't be too far away. Granger wasn't that big of a town.

We sat there on the steps of the tri-level with our friend, Judy, who was showing us the house. Ben said, "I don't know. I just feel like our family is supposed to live here." The sun was streaming in through the front bay window making patterns of light on the wall. Much like the same light that poured in through my bedroom window the morning after I found Jesus to be so faithful, holding me tight throughout my darkest night. My heart was brimming with peace. We made an offer, and it was immediately accepted.

My mom called one afternoon when I was packing up boxes on New York Street, "Nikki, what did you say the name of that church is that you want to attend?"

"It's Harvest in Granger," I told her.

"You need to go look at a map," she said, "I think it is just on the other side of your neighborhood!"

I couldn't believe it. We were in such a hurry to find a house during that one weekend that we hadn't even checked where the church actually was. I quickly googled the location, and there it was. Just beyond the interweaving streets with a cornfield in its backyard was our new church, all within walking distance of our new home.

> *"The heart of man plans his way,*
> *but the Lord establishes his steps." (Proverbs 16:9)*

Bowed Down to the Dust

*The reason Reese stamped her foot and declared,
"This is not close to my cousins!"*

Bowed Down to the Dust

The night she held Lyndi's hand and cried, "But Lyndi, I am going to miss you so much."

Finally home on Tally Ho Drive in South Bend, eagerly awaiting company!

Bowed Down to the Dust

The Ending

Standing on this mountaintop
Looking just how far we've come
Knowing that for every step
You were with us

Kneeling on this battle ground
Seeing just how much You've done
Knowing every victory
Was your power in us

Scars and struggles on the way
But with joy our hearts can say
Yes, our hearts can say

Never once did we ever walk alone
Never once did You leave us on our own
You are faithful, God, You are faithful[2]

---

[2]- Jason Ingram/Matt Redman/Tim Wanstall, Never Once lyrics © Spirit Music Group, BMG Rights Management, Essential Music Publishing.

Bowed Down to the Dust

It was a popular song in the spring of 2013; but even so, I felt like the Lord had it written and sung on that day just for us to be able to sing back to Him. Ben and I held hands and sang our hearts out to the Lord. It was our last Sunday with our church body before we moved home and started our new lives in South Bend. Our hearts were heavy and light. *Ah*, the paradox life can so often be!

We said goodbye to many people. We shed many tears. We went forward at the end of the service one last time for prayer. One of our pastors laid his hands on both of us and prayed a blessing over our family, "Lord, I ask that wherever you take these servants that they would be used by you. Make Ben's gifts immediately known to his new church and use him for your glory." Before walking away, he looked Ben in the eyes and said, "Sometimes God just moves us to a new place to uncover things that lay dormant elsewhere."

We finished packing up the rental that week, loaded up the moving truck, and drove home to Indiana for good! We joked that Ben had just graduated from the seminary of life. Aside from all the many situations that tested and refined our faith, he had another perk from all his long days of scrubbing carpets clean. It was a solitary job and perfectly acceptable to plug into devices while you did your work. My husband had logged thousands of hours listening to sermons by great Gospel-centered preachers over the course of the past 3 1/2 years. It might not have been the pastor's college in Maryland that he was hoping to attend, but it was surely enough to add up to some sort of a seminary level education!

The next few weeks were a blur of starting a new job and getting settled into our new home. We attended the church in Granger once while we were waiting to close on our house; but now that we were here as full-time residents, we were excited to immediately get involved. I recall pulling out of the parking lot one Sunday morning and saying to Ben, "I guess you truly are laying down ministry. There are 600 people in this church. Even if you are gifted, how would they ever see that? And I'm sure there are a lot of other gifted men here too."

Bowed Down to the Dust

"I just want my family to thrive, and I want to raise my kids in a solid, Gospel- centered church," he replied. "I will trust the Lord to give me contentment if I am cleaning carpets the rest of my life."

The next week we had a meeting scheduled with Matt Mendenhall, one of the pastors on staff. As new attenders, and looking to become members quickly, Ben wanted to meet with a pastor and ask some questions about the church. The two started talking about small groups, and Ben shared from his heart everything that small groups meant to him.

Matt leaned back in his chair and said, "Wait a second, were you at the training I just did for small group leaders last weekend?"

Ben said, "Oh, no, we were still unpacking the house."

Matt put his feet down on the floor, leaned forward, and with his elbows resting on his knees said, "You are speaking back to me everything that I have been trying to teach our people. Do you have any desire to become a pastor again? We really need to hire a pastor to lead our small groups."

Nine months later Ben began his full-time position at Harvest Bible Chapel* in Granger, Indiana, as pastor of Adult Ministries and Small Groups. He resigned from his position at the water restoration company where he had quickly moved up. His boss accepted his resignation but said, "We were just about to offer you a promotion with a company car and no on-call time. Do you want to know what the salary would have been?" Ben thanked him, but wisely answered no. The Lord had taken Ben on a unique journey to prepare and equip him for the good works that He had prepared in advance for him to do, and a company car along with a manager's salary could not outshine the call of God.

Ben began his pastoral duties, and on many days would let the car sit idle in the garage as he chose to walk past the rows of houses, along the curved streets with the sunlight streaming through the tree branches only to arrive at his office within the church building that was essentially behind our home. Sometimes the kids and I would ride our bikes to bring him lunch or just to greet him and the other staff members. When he needed to work a little later at times or had

Bowed Down to the Dust

a counseling appointment in the evening, it was my utter joy to release him. My heart had been trained in advance, by many late on-call jobs, for the good works the Lord had for me to do too.

The devotion entry I read the week we moved out of Tonti Street and started this grand adventure had proven true. We had fought through so much mist for the past 3 1/2 years, but Jesus had truly been there as the rock beneath our feet. We may go through long seasons of seemingly being bowed down to the dust, but His steadfast love and faithfulness endures forever, even when all we see are the glimpses.

Finding no way to a city to dwell in;
Hungry and thirsty,
Their soul fainted within them,
Then they cried to the Lord in their trouble,
And he delivered them from their distress.
He led them by a straight way
Till they reached a city to dwell in.
Let them thank the Lord for His steadfast love,
For His wondrous works to the children of man!
For he satisfies the longing soul,
And the hungry soul he fills with good things.

Psalm 107:4-9

*Renamed Gospel City Church

Bowed Down to the Dust

Our second Easter on staff at Gospel City prior to the birth of our twins!

Bowed Down to the Dust

Ben, reading about the Man of Sorrows in Isaiah 53.

In 2019, Ben went through the Send Network Assessment for church planting hosted by a church in Aurora. He knew the building well; it was one of the places he logged time listening to sermons years before while cleaning their carpets.

Acknowledgments

To the Lord, the Giver of the gifts, thank you for redeeming me and extending your long-suffering patience to me. Thank you for your afflictions. You know how to keep my heart. "Whom have I in heaven but you? And there is nothing on earth that I desire besides you." Psalm 73:25

To my husband, Ben, you have been my best friend and favorite person for over 18 years now and have taught me to trust the Lord more than anyone else I know. I am *honored* to be your wife. I love you; and I love walking through this life, with all of its trials, by your side.

To my five children: Reese Nicole, Isaac Benjamin, Raegan Lenee, Harper Jean, and Hudson Joshua, you have your mother's whole heart. I love being your mom and desire nothing more than to see you seek joy in the Lord, who is worthy of all our praise.

To the Kaufman and Hurt families, even if you weren't all mentioned by name in this little book, you have all impacted our lives in many ways. We are thankful to God for our families and that we get to do ministry in a place that isn't too far away from any of you.

Bowed Down to the Dust

To the Segers, you have been some of our dearest friends for many years now. Thank you for opening your very first home to near strangers. We continue to reap the blessing of your kindness to this day. Praise God you saw all Indiana has to offer, and you found your way home too. Thankfully, it just happened to be around the corner from us again.

To my publisher, Marty Duren at Missional Press, thank you for your encouragement to keep writing my vignettes and for believing that at least one person might desire to read this story! To my editor, Kristen Dobson, thank you for your friendship and using your giftedness to make my words better! Your attention to detail is astounding. I am grateful.

To all the local churches we have been called to: Calvary Baptist in South Bend, IN, Redeemer Community in Aurora, IL, Gospel City in Granger, IN, and now Gospel Community in Goshen, IN, you have all been places of solace for us. We are delighted that the call on our lives has been to the local church. There is no other place we'd rather be. We gladly lay down our lives to pursue Christ with you!

Bowed Down to the Dust

www.ingramcontent.com/pod-product-compliance
Lightning Source LLC
Chambersburg PA
CBHW072207100526
44589CB00015B/2402